The Pledge of Allegiance

CORNERSTONES
OF FREEDOM™

SECOND SERIES

Christine Webster

Children's Press®
A Division of Scholastic Inc.
New York • Toronto • London • Auckland • Sydney
Mexico City • New Delhi • Hong Kong
Danbury, Connecticut

Photographs © 2003: AP/Wide World Photos: 32 (Shawn Baldwin), cover bottom, 34 (Seth Perlman), 24 (Bill Zimmer); Brown Brothers: 20 bottom; Corbis Images: 5, 7, 11, 13, 15, 20 inset, 44 top left (Bettmann), 28, 45 left (Russell Lee), 37 (Wally McNamee), 29 (Susan Ragan/Reuters NewMedia Inc.); Getty Images: 33 (Ron Sachs), 35 (Mario Tama); ImageState/Peter Langone: 22; North Wind Picture Archives: 4, 44 top right; Photo Researchers, NY: 36 (George Jones III), 16, 44 bottom (Rafael Macia), 25 (Mary Evans Picture Library); PhotoEdit: cover top, 3, 40, 41 (Vic Bider), 30 (Gary Connor), 38 (Spencer Grant); Stock Boston/Peter Southwick: 19; Stock Montage, Inc.: 17; The Image Works: 27 (Randi Aglin/Syracuse Newspapers), 9, 45 right (Rob Crandall), 31 (Alan Tannenbaum), 8 (Topham).

XNR Productions: Map on page 12

Library of Congress Cataloging-in-Publication Data

Webster, Christine.
The Pledge of Allegiance / Christine Webster.
    p. cm.—(Cornerstones of freedom. Second series)
  Summary: Discusses the history and meaning of the Pledge of Allegiance, which was first published in *The Youth's Companion* in 1892 as part of a campaign to promote patriotism led by James B. Upham and Francis Bellamy.
  Includes bibliographical references and index.
  ISBN 0-516-22674-6
  1. Bellamy, Francis. Pledge of Allegiance to the Flag—History—Juvenile literature.
2. Upham, James B.—Juvenile literature. [1. Pledge of Allegiance. 2. Upham, James B.
3. Bellamy, Francis. 4. Patriotism.] I. Title. II. Series.
JC346 .W42 2003
323.6'5'0973—dc21

                                          2002009024

1 2 3 4 5 6 7 8 9 10 R 12 11 10 09 08 07 06 05 04 03

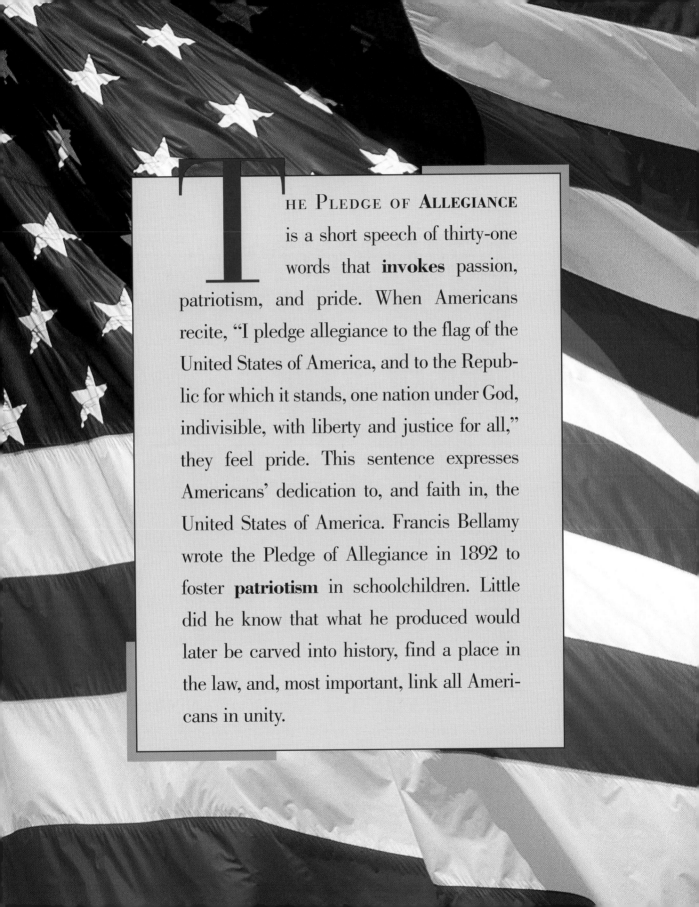

THE PLEDGE OF **ALLEGIANCE** is a short speech of thirty-one words that **invokes** passion, patriotism, and pride. When Americans recite, "I pledge allegiance to the flag of the United States of America, and to the Republic for which it stands, one nation under God, indivisible, with liberty and justice for all," they feel pride. This sentence expresses Americans' dedication to, and faith in, the United States of America. Francis Bellamy wrote the Pledge of Allegiance in 1892 to foster **patriotism** in schoolchildren. Little did he know that what he produced would later be carved into history, find a place in the law, and, most important, link all Americans in unity.

Women march proudly for equal rights and voting rights at a parade in 1911. Women had been marching in parades like this since the late 1800s.

THE YOUTH'S COMPANION

The United States in the 1800s was much different than the United States we know today. Many of the things taken for granted now did not even exist then: email, telephones, cars, or even electricity. The lack of these modern conveniences

* * * *

did not stop the United States from eventually developing into the country it is today. In fact, the United States we know today was shaped by events that took place during the nineteenth century.

Under President Thomas Jefferson's leadership, the United States expanded westward as a group of explorers led by Meriwether Lewis and William Clark opened the Pacific Northwest for thousands of pioneers. Women's rights movements emerged. Many people believed women should have a more important role in society, and be given the right to work in jobs reserved exclusively for men as well as the right to vote. The 19th amendment to the Constitution finally gave women the right to vote in 1920. Railroad track was laid down across the United States, making it easier to travel and transport goods. Before and during the Civil War, a railroad of a very different kind was operating: the Underground Railroad, a series of safe "stations" to conceal escaped **slaves** and help them reach freedom.

The 1800s was also a time when Americans disagreed over many issues. When Abraham Lincoln was elected president in 1860, the United States was in a state of turmoil. From

Abraham Lincoln (1809 to 1865) studied and practiced law for over twenty years until he joined the Republican Party in 1855. He became the 16th president of the United States in 1860 and a great leader in American history. He was shot at Ford's theater in 1865.

5

the earliest days of the United States, there were cultural and economic differences between the Southern and Northern states. As the century went on, the North was developing an economy based on industry and manufacturing. Meanwhile, the South remained a region whose economy was based on agriculture, with the most important crop being cotton.

Many Americans in the Southern states owned slaves of African descent. This meant that they owned another human being who was forced to work for them. The Southern states believed slavery was necessary to their way of life—especially after the invention of the cotton gin, when their economy became more dependent on this crop. The Northern states wanted to prevent the spread of slavery to the Western territories, and some Northerners wanted all the slaves to be freed. With the election of Abraham Lincoln, a Northerner, the Southern states began to **secede,** and eventually eleven Southern states set up their own separate government and elected their own president.

Shortly after the Southern states formed the Confederate States of America, known as the Confederacy, the Civil War broke out. The North and South battled for four terrible years. This was the first and only time one section of the United States fought a war against another section. At the end of the bloody war in 1865, the South was defeated and the institution of slavery came to an end in the United States. Despite the Civil War and the tragic loss of life, Americans were once again united as citizens of the same nation. The eleven states of the former Confederacy took an oath of loyalty and reentered the Union.

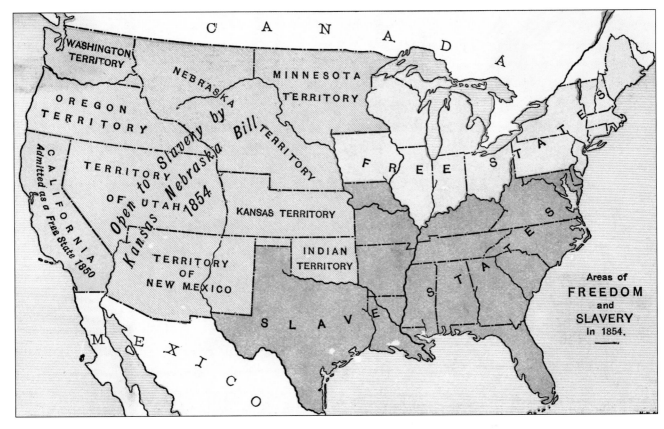

This map shows how the country was divided into free and slave states before the Civil War, as well as the territories that remained undecided.

With the Civil War still a vivid and painful memory for Americans, a magazine executive named James Bailey Upham wanted to restore the level of patriotism, or loyalty and love for one's country, that he felt Americans once shared but was now **waning.** He believed that in order to raise the level of patriotism in the United States, one should start with schoolchildren, who were generally innocent and eager to believe in something. In 1888, Upham had an idea: increase children's interest in the American flag, and you would increase their feelings of patriotism.

★ ★ ★ ★

Emily Dickinson (1830 to 1886) was born in Amherst, Massachusetts. Though unknown during her lifetime, she is now regarded as one of the greatest American poets.

FAMOUS CONTRIBUTORS

Contributors to *The Youth's Companion* included poet Emily Dickinson, whose work was published after her death, and Presidents Theodore Roosevelt and Grover Cleveland.

Born in 1845 in New Hampshire, James Upham worked for a Boston magazine called *The Youth's Companion.* Upham worked for his uncle-by-marriage and the owner of the magazine, Daniel Ford. *The Youth's Companion* magazine circulated once a week to approximately half a million homes around the United States. It was a leading family magazine and has been compared to today's *Reader's Digest.* It was geared toward children but also contained many informative articles for adults to enjoy. The magazine was filled with adventure stories, articles, and puzzles.

RENEWING PATRIOTISM

As a first step toward achieving his goal, Upham decided to sell American flags to public schools all across the United States. Thus, the

School Flag Movement was born. Advertisements and articles relating to the American flag appeared throughout *The Youth's Companion* and managed to reach the homes of hundreds of thousands of children. Students could write to the magazine and request one hundred cards that they could then sell for ten cents apiece. On each card was written, "This Certificate entitles the holder to one share in the patriotic influence of a flag over the schoolhouse." Once the students in a school earned ten dollars from the sale of these cards, they could buy an American flag for their school from the magazine. Upham also captured children's interest by holding contests in the magazine. For example, there were essay contests. The student who wrote the best essay in each state won a huge free flag for his or her school. That particular flag measured 9 feet (2.7 m) high by 15 feet (4.5 m) wide. Upham also encouraged patriotism by selling other items, such as patriotic pictures to be hung on school walls. The magazine encouraged girls to form a "Mending the Flag" society. The first ten schools that formed a society to mend their flags received a free kit to help with the sewing.

A young girl performs the proper way to do the Pledge of Allegiance with the right hand over her heart.

Eventually the School Flag Movement was recognized by the United States government. In fact, by 1895 the first flag law was passed in Massachusetts making it **obligatory,** or mandatory, for school officials to provide a flag for each schoolhouse. In the following years, many more states would pass similar flag laws.

By 1891 twenty-five thousand schools had purchased American flags and hung them proudly over their school-houses. In schools across the country, children cheered when the American flag was raised. Foreign-born children and parents new to America were greatly moved by the sight of the symbol of the United States flying over schoolhouses.

There was a renewed sense of patriotism in the country, but Upham felt that still more could be done. How could he raise these feelings to a new level? The World's Columbian Exposition gave James Upham another idea.

The previous year, Congress had passed a **declaration** establishing the World's Columbian Exposition. The theme of this event was the discovery of the Americas by Italian explorer Christopher Columbus. Columbus sailed west across the Atlantic Ocean in search of a route from Europe to Asia. Instead, he discovered the Americas in 1492.

The World's Columbian Exposition was going to be held in Chicago, Illinois, in 1892. That year marked the four-hundredth anniversary of Columbus's discovery. Because of the new interest in the American flag, the celebration gave Upham the idea of introducing a flag salute.

A national committee of educators and civic leaders got together and planned a public school celebration for

Explorer Christopher
Columbus kneels as he
comes ashore on Hispaniola,
the island in the Caribbean
where he landed during his
first voyage to the New
World in 1492.

Columbus Day. In 1892, *The Youth's Companion* joined in
the campaign to promote the National Public School Celebration for Columbus Day. The focal point of the celebration
would be the newly purchased flags and a salute (not yet
written) to this great American symbol.

Upham began furiously promoting the idea of the Public School Celebration. Daniel Ford assigned Upham and
a colleague, Francis Bellamy, to work together on the
celebration. Upham explained to Bellamy that he wanted
to come up with a flag salute for Columbus Day. He

described for Bellamy the type of salute he had in mind. They began their work: planning the Public School Celebration and thinking of an appropriate salute to the great American flag.

WHO WAS FRANCIS BELLAMY?

Francis Bellamy was born in Mount Morris, New York, on May 18, 1855. Mount Morris is located 45 miles south of Lake Ontario and the city of Rochester, in Livingston County. In 1859, Bellamy's family moved to Rome, New York, about 150 miles to the northeast, where Francis Bellamy was raised.

This map shows the location of Mt. Morris, New York, where Francis Bellamy was born

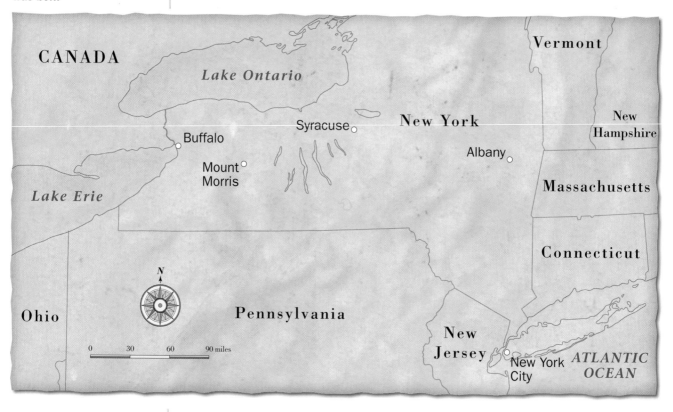

Francis Bellamy's father was a minister at a Baptist church. Bellamy shared his father's interest in religion and entered the Rochester **Theological Seminary** in 1876 to study to become a Baptist minister. He began his ministry four years later at the Baptist Church of Little Falls, New York. In 1885 he left the church in Little Falls to preach at the Dearborn Street Church in Boston.

This calendar was distributed to thousands of homes compliments of *The Youth's Companion.*

Bellamy believed in socialism. Socialism is a political system in which the state controls the production and distribution of goods. He also believed it was the duty of the government to help people who worked hard. He thought this was the main purpose of a government. He wanted to use the power of government to make people's lives better. He was noted for his socialist and patriotic beliefs.

In 1891, Daniel Ford began attending Bellamy's church in Boston. Ford loved the way Bellamy could express himself so clearly in his sermons. The two men became very close friends. Ford felt that Bellamy's ability to express his ideas would be a great asset to his magazine. One day Ford approached his friend. Bellamy liked what Ford was saying.

Francis Bellamy had been under pressure from his church to resign because of his socialist opinions. When this new opportunity presented itself in 1891, he finally left the church and went to work for his friend at *The Youth's Companion.*

Daniel Ford had his nephew and Bellamy work together as a team on the Public School Celebration. Their main goal was to come up with a flag salute. Both Upham and Bellamy hoped to make the new salute to the flag a year-round occurrence and one of national pride.

Francis Bellamy once remarked that he envisioned flags flying over every school and public building from coast to coast. What greater way to unify a country? Both Upham and Bellamy believed that children around the United States were becoming very enthusiastic about honoring these symbols in their schools.

Bellamy worked very hard to prepare for the Public School Celebration. He was appointed chairman of the National Education Association's (NEA) executive committee for the Columbus Day celebration. The NEA agreed to support *The Youth's Companion* in any way they could. Francis Bellamy gained the cooperation and support of educators, newspapers, and many government officials. In fact, Bellamy traveled to the state capitol to meet with President Benjamin Harrison, the twenty-third president of the United States. He managed to convince President Harrison to proclaim the Public School Celebration the focal point of the World's Columbian Exposition. He even campaigned for Columbus Day to become a national holiday to be celebrated each year on October 12.

A PROCLAMATION AND A VISION

In *The Youth's Companion,* Bellamy published the proclamation signed by President Benjamin Harrison that read, "Let the flag float over every schoolhouse in the land and the exercise be such as shall impress upon our youth the patriotic duty of citizenship."

* * * *

President Benjamin Harrison (1833 to 1901) was born in Ohio as the grandson of the ninth president of the United States, William Henry Harrison. Benjamin Harrison studied law and later became the 23rd president of the United States in 1888.

COLUMBUS DAY EXERCISES

A typical Columbus Day exercise in 1892 began with a 9 A.M. school assembly during which the president's message was read, the flag was raised, and the new salute was recited. This was followed by a prayer and the singing of "My Country, 'Tis of Thee."

Upham and Bellamy worked together closely on a detailed program of exercises for the celebration. Francis Bellamy did the actual writing of the program. *The Youth's Companion* published the program in the September 8, 1892, edition. Hundreds of thousands of children across the nation were able to participate in the Columbus Day

Forty-second Street, New York City. Americans all over the United States show their pride by hanging American flags up and down their streets.

AN EARLIER SALUTE

In 1889 there was only one well-known American flag salute. A principal of a New York kindergarten, Colonel George T. Balch, wrote it for Flag Day in New York. It read: "We give our heads and our hearts to God and our country: one country, one language, one flag."

Southern citizens take the "Oath of Allegiance" to regain their citizenship and political rights in the United States following the Civil War.

celebration, reading the exercises printed in their own copies of the magazine.

Both Upham and Bellamy thought hard about this new salute. They both agreed that the new salute needed to be more like a vow of loyalty to the flag. Upham put his pen to paper and wrote many versions of a salute. Unfortunately, he was never satisfied with any of them. He just could not find the right words. Eventually, he turned over the responsibility of writing the entire salute to Bellamy.

THE PLEDGE OF ALLEGIANCE

Francis Bellamy felt that a pledge, or vow, would be more appropriate than a salute to the flag. He remembered that during the Civil War many Southern states had to take an "Oath of Allegiance" to regain their political rights in the

Union. Bellamy liked the word allegiance. He decided that his version of a salute to the flag would be a "pledge of allegiance" rather than a salute.

The Civil War also stirred up many emotions in Bellamy that brought certain words to mind: *one nation, indivisible,* and *liberty.* He realized that although state had fought against state, in the end they remained united. The United States must always remain *indivisible.* Bellamy also thought of the freed slaves and how all Americans now had the right to freedom, or *liberty.* With these thoughts and words in mind, Francis Bellamy set out to write the Pledge of Allegiance. He finished the salute to the American flag in August of 1892. The pledge was only one sentence long and contained a mere twenty-two words, but together they were powerful. It went as follows: "I pledge allegiance to my Flag and the Republic for which it stands: one Nation indivisible, with Liberty and Justice for all." Francis Bellamy called it the Pledge of Allegiance.

Bellamy showed his newly written pledge to Upham. Upham loved it, but felt they should combine the spoken salute with some sort of gesture or hand salute to make it complete. To demonstrate what he had in mind, Upham stretched out his right arm with the palm of his hand facing down. He kept his arm raised while he recited the new pledge. The two men were very pleased with their combined efforts. The completed Pledge of Allegiance was ready to be presented to the National Education Association committee and to Daniel Ford.

* * * *

Ford and the rest of the committee loved the Pledge of Allegiance as well, and it was approved. They all agreed that it honored the American flag and would help unify the country. The only thing that was insisted upon was that the author remain **anonymous,** or unknown, since that was the policy of *The Youth's Companion.*

In October of 1892 the word *to* was added to the pledge: ". . . and to the republic . . ." This brought the total number of words to twenty-three.

The Pledge of Allegiance was published for the first time on September 8, 1892, in *The Youth's Companion,* along with the exercises for the Columbus Day celebration. Hundreds of thousands of schoolchildren across the United States read

The flag has long been a symbol of patriotism. Here, a modern-day family in Lexington, Massachusetts, shows their support for the United States by painting an American flag across their house.

the new pledge in the magazine. The words made them think of their country and honored its symbol, the American flag. Patriotism was on the rise once again.

The first time the Pledge of Allegiance was recited was in New York City on Columbus Day, October 12, 1892, during the National Public School Celebration. Upham wanted to impress upon the nation that public schools were the greatest achievement of America since its discovery four hundred years earlier. So on this day, thirty-five thousand schoolchildren marched along Fifth Avenue. The students stopped and stood proud, gave the American flag a salute—right

Henry Ford (1863 to 1947) was born in Dearborn, Michigan, and pioneered automobile manufacturing. He built his first automobile in 1896 and continued to produce them into the 1920s. The automobile shown on the right is an example of how Ford's cars looked in the 1920s as automobiles became increasingly popular and changed transportation in the United States forever.

hand lifted, palm downward—and, together as one, recited the words of the Pledge of Allegiance.

Over sixty thousand public schools around the United States participated in the National Public School Celebration for Columbus Day. Twelve million students proudly recited the new salute to their newly purchased flags. The Pledge of Allegiance was a great success. The words perfectly expressed what many Americans felt about their nation. Soon the Pledge of Allegiance became a morning ritual in schools across the nation.

CHANGES TO THE PLEDGE

By the 1920s, not only was the Pledge of Allegiance in for some changes but the country, too, was changing rapidly. Wilbur and Orville Wright had made the first successful flight of a motor-powered airplane. Automobiles raced along the roads as Henry Ford's assembly-line process made cars available to the average American. The Model T Ford automobile sold all over the United States for the price of $950. Radio stations began broadcasting across the country. Women had won the right to vote in 1920, and many whites were showing interest in African-American culture. Jazz clubs were popping up all over the country. The United States, itself, had also grown. Forty-eight states were now part of the American Union. The total population of the United States had reached 106 million people.

EQUALITY

Francis Bellamy considered using the word *equality* in his pledge, but Bellamy, along with the state superintendents of education and his committee, was against equality for certain minorities.

21

Military and police personnel proudly salute the American flag.

By 1923 the Pledge of Allegiance was thirty-one years old. Not once had the words that Francis Bellamy wrote been changed. Now some people felt that it was time for the pledge to be revised.

The American Legion, started in 1919, was an organization of United States war veterans. They held a national meeting, called the National Flag Conference, on June 14, 1923. It was held in the country's capital, Washington, D.C. The conference, the first of its kind, was **convened** to discuss all matters regarding the American flag. The conference participants drafted the first Flag Code. The code established a set of rules regarding the proper display of and respect for flags owned by **civilians.** A civilian is a person who is not on active duty in a military, police, or fire-fighting organization. The conference also discussed the aging Pledge of Allegiance.

The American Legion felt the words *my flag* in the Pledge of Allegiance could refer to a flag from any country. They were worried that perhaps children and adults born in other countries might think of their native lands when reciting the original words of the pledge. The Pledge of Allegiance was written for Americans and about the United States only. The committee made a decision to change the pledge. They wanted to replace the words *my flag* with *the flag of the United States.*

Francis Bellamy did not like the change, but he had no choice. The first National Flag Conference resulted in the addition of four words to the Pledge of Allegiance. One year later the words *of America* were also added. Now the pledge contained six more words than the original version, and no more changes would be incorporated into the pledge for decades to come.

WHO IS THE TRUE AUTHOR?

Over the years many wondered who was the original author of the Pledge of Allegiance. Was it Francis Bellamy or James Bailey Upham? What gave rise to this mystery was the insistence of *The Youth's Companion* that the author of the pledge remain anonymous. Determining the authorship of the pledge was difficult.

Francis Bellamy passed away in 1931 at the age of seventy-six. His family felt that they had enough evidence to

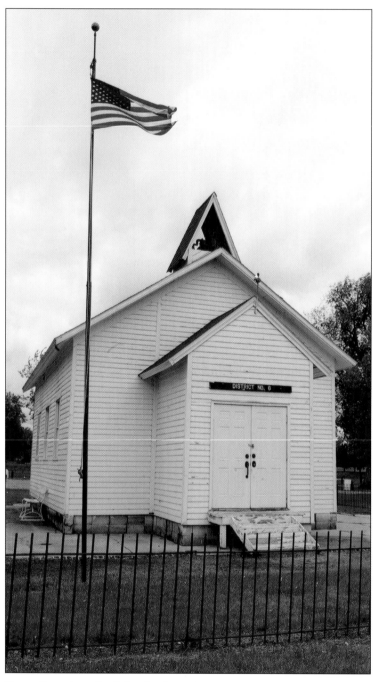

No matter what size it is, the flag of the United States flies over every public school in the country.

prove that he was the author of the Pledge. Upham's family made similar claims on his behalf. Unfortunately, it was difficult to determine who should get credit for the pledge. James B. Upham was responsible for American flags flying over schools across the country, and he thought of the idea to recite a flag salute in public schools and at public ceremonies. It was evident that he was a central figure in the creation of the pledge of Allegiance.

On the other hand, Francis Bellamy helped **campaign** to make Columbus Day a holiday. He was responsible for the actual writing of the Public School Celebration exercises and he was the chairman of the committee that planned and organized the celebration. Most importantly, Francis Bellamy was the one who actually thought of the original twenty-three words and put pen to paper.

It was still a tough decision to make. In 1939 a committee, called the United States Flag Association, was appointed to determine who was the author of the Pledge of Allegiance. They carefully weighed all the evidence and held a vote. The committee voted **unanimously**. They all believed that Bellamy was the sole author of the Pledge of Allegiance. The pledge contained the words of Francis Bellamy, so only he would be recognized as the author.

FINAL CHANGES

In October of 1942 the Pledge of Allegiance was fifty years old. It was engraved in the minds of, and loved by, Americans across the United States. In order to prevent the loss of this pledge of patriotism, Congress decided to make the Pledge of Allegiance an official part of the Flag Code of the United States. Now only the president could make changes to it. The Pledge of Allegiance would live forever in history as an official document of the United States.

Originally, the recitation of the pledge was accompanied by a salute that consisted of holding the right arm out, palm down. When German dictator Adolf Hitler came to power in Europe during World War II, some Americans were concerned that this position of the arm and hand resembled his **Nazi** salute. It made many people uncomfortable, so it was agreed that the salute

Adolf Hitler, who ruled Germany as a dictator from 1933 to 1945, performs the Nazi salute. Fearful that the salute performed with the Pledge of Allegiance resembled the Nazi salute, Congress changed it in 1942.

INDIVIDUAL FREEDOM AND THE PLEDGE

One year later, in 1943, the Supreme Court ruled that it was unconstitutional to force someone to recite the pledge. To do so would contradict the meaning of the words *liberty and justice for all* and violate the First Amendment to the Constitution.

needed to be changed. In 1942, Congress decided that the pledge should be recited while holding the right hand over the heart.

The pledge came under scrutiny once again in 1954. Earlier, in 1952, a Roman Catholic organization called the Knights of Columbus had sent to the White House a proposed amendment to the pledge. They requested that the words *under God* follow the words *one nation* in the Pledge of Allegiance. They reasoned that these words would serve to remind Americans that their country needed to be not just physically strong, but spiritually strong as well. In 1954 the change was accepted. The Pledge of Allegiance was now a patriotic oath and a public prayer. It had gained eight words in sixty-two years and read, "I pledge allegiance to the flag of the United States of America and to the Republic for which it stands, one Nation under God, indivisible, with liberty and justice for all."

WHAT DOES THE PLEDGE OF ALLEGIANCE MEAN?

In 1892, Francis Bellamy thought about what Americans would want to say when thinking of the American flag and their country. He carefully chose each word in the pledge to express these sentiments. Through the years, the changes to the original Pledge of Allegiance have incorporated what later generations wanted to include. Some words or groups of words in the Pledge of Allegiance can still be

The Knights of Columbus marching in uniform. It was a request from this organization that got the words "under God" added to the Pledge of Allegiance.

tricky for children to make sense of. When the pledge is broken down and explained, it is simple to understand.

When you *pledge allegiance,* you are making a promise to be true or loyal to something. In this case, when you recite the words *I pledge allegiance to the flag,* you are promising to be true to your country and its national symbol. The American flag is a symbol that represents the

★ ★ ★ ★

United States of America. The words *of the United States of America* recognize each state that has joined the union to make the United States a country. They are also a reminder of the country you are promising to be loyal to. With these words, all citizens, including foreign-born citizens, are pledging to be true to the United States.

The word *republic* refers to the form of government in the United States. A republic is a type of government in which people elect representatives from among themselves to make laws. The head of the government is not a dictator or monarch.

Men saying the pledge with their hats removed and placed over their left shoulders at a baseball game in Vale, Oregon, on July 4, 1941.

* * * *

TO SAY THE PLEDGE OR NOT?

No student or teacher is required to participate in the recitation of the Pledge of Allegiance because of the First Amendment to the Constitution that protects his or her right to freedom of speech. This guarantees freedom of expression to citizens of the United States. If students choose not to join in the recitation of the pledge, they cannot be punished for their choice and are asked to stay seated, quietly.

Michael Newdow didn't like students at his five-year-old daughter's school standing up for the Pledge of Allegiance each morning. In June 2002 he challenged the pledge by saying that the phrase "under God" violated the U.S. Constitution. He said it broke the law separating church and state. The courts agreed with him, going even farther than in the 1943 case (*West Virginia State Board of Education v. Barnette*).

The words *for which it stands* are talking about the flag. Again they say the flag symbolizes the country. *One nation* means our country is united, and *under God* suggests a country in which people are free to believe in a supreme being or creator of the earth.

Indivisible means that the country cannot be divided. The Civil War was fought to uphold this principle. The country remained indivisible.

The final words, *with liberty and justice for all,* mean that everyone has the right to freedom and that each person should receive fair and equal treatment and be governed by the same set of laws. So in short, the Pledge of Allegiance is a promise to be loyal to the United States and also a reminder of the principles the nation is based on.

Unlike civilian men, military men do not remove their hats while saluting the flag.

The Pledge of Allegiance should be recited while standing at attention facing the flag, with the right hand over the heart. Fingers should be together and horizontal. Men should remove their hats. Military personnel in uniform should face the flag and give a military salute. After the final words are spoken—*justice for all*—the arm should drop to the side.

THE PLEDGE OF ALLEGIANCE AND SEPTEMBER 11, 2001

On Tuesday, September 11, 2001, the United States of America came under attack. A group of terrorists hijacked American airplanes and crashed them into the World Trade Center in New York, the Pentagon in Arlington, Virginia, and an empty field in Pennsylvania. Soon after

Smoke billows from the World Trade Center twin towers on September 11, 2001, during the horrific terrorist attacks.

Debris from the twin towers covers Ground Zero as firefighters and rescue workers search for victims.

takeoff, the terrorists took control of the planes. They used the airplanes as bombs to destroy their intended targets. The outcome was devastating. Nearly three thousand people were killed as a result of this horrific attack, and thousands more were injured. The whole world was affected.

Following the events of September 11, 2001, reciting the Pledge of Allegiance became a source of comfort to many Americans. Citizens, overcome by a feeling of powerlessness, needed a way to express their love for their country and desire to defend it. Reciting the Pledge of Allegiance and singing patriotic songs were ways of demonstrating to the terrorists that the United States was still strong and still united.

Following September 11, people demonstrated their support and patriotism in many ways. They came from all over the country to Ground Zero, site of the World Trade Center disaster, to help in any way they could. People showed their support by holding memorial services and donating blood in every little town and big city across the country. Concerts and other fund-raisers were held to raise money for the victims' families. Americans attended sports events, at the urging of public officials, to show the terrorists they could not disrupt the American way of life. Huge American flags were displayed on baseball and football fields. At these events the heroes of September 11, the firefighters and police officers,

Josh Groban (left) sings the national anthem as U.S. Secretary of State Colin Powell (second from the right) and representatives of the New York Police Department and the Fire Department of New York salute at the "Concert for America" on September 9, 2002, held at the John F. Kennedy Center for the Performing Arts in Washington, D.C.

were given the honor of leading the Pledge of Allegiance and singing the national anthem. Many Americans watched the events on television and experienced the feeling that "we are all in this together—one country." The tragedy affected all Americans, not just New Yorkers, Washingtonians, and Pennsylvanians.

Perhaps the most moving moment came when people across the country watched on television as a few New York City firefighters, in an act of patriotism and defiance, raised a tattered flag, which had been found in the midst of the chaos and destruction, over mangled steel beams that had once been the twin towers.

A group of children say the Pledge of Allegiance during their early morning ritual at school.

* * * *

Two beams of light representing the twin towers shoot into the night sky shortly after the September 11 attacks.

35

Patriotism was high after September 11, and even though it violates the Flag Code, more and more people wore clothes decorated with the flag.

★ ★ ★ ★

Before September 11, many students did not find it "cool" to stand up and recite the pledge or display any feelings of patriotism, so they chose to sit out during their school's morning ritual. Following September 11, many realized how precious their freedom was and how they felt about preserving it. Now many of the students who had not participated in the recitation are standing tall and speaking the words, committed to memory long ago, with new understanding. When they place their hands over their hearts, they are reciting the pledge with a renewed sense of allegiance to their country. They believe in the words they are saying and experience feelings of pride in being an American.

Once again feelings of patriotism are running high, just as they were over one hundred years ago when James Upham and Francis Bellamy were working on the Pledge of Allegiance for the Public School Celebration. After September 11, many stores could not keep up with the demands from the public for the American flag as they scrambled to replace their stock. Citizens, businesses, and neighboring countries

* * * *

all wanted to display the symbol of the United States in a show of unity and support.

Now, not only do American flags wave from schoolhouses and government buildings, but they also decorate cars, stores, and even people. The American flag has become a fashion statement, even though technically it violates the Flag Code, as people wear clothing decorated with the flag. The Fourth of

THE FLAG AND THE ANTHEM

The United States is the only country with a national anthem dedicated to its flag as well as a verbal salute or pledge.

Children dressed in American attire and carrying American flags. American flags were in high demand after the events of September 11.

37

★ ★ ★ ★

The American flag flies over the White House, the home of the President of the United States of America.

* * * *

July used to be the main day of the year to celebrate American patriotism, but now, displays of patriotism are seen every day.

The Pledge of Allegiance gives people hope in times of danger. It also gives them strength in times of peace. On October 12, 2001, over one hundred years from the first time the pledge was recited, children across the United States paused to pledge allegiance once again. At two o'clock in the afternoon on Columbus Day, one month after the horrific attacks on the United States, the nation simultaneously recited the Pledge of Allegiance. Even President George W. Bush took time to recite the pledge from the Oval Office at the White House. This event gave children a chance to participate in a nationwide display of pride and patriotism. As in 1892, the Pledge of Allegiance once again gave Americans an opportunity to vow their loyalty to their flag and their country.

September 11, 2001, has proven that the United States is still indivisible. Americans vow their loyalty to their country every day—some by reciting the pledge, others with unspoken feelings in their minds and hearts—and are doing everything they can to fight terrorism in order to protect their freedom. When Americans began pledging allegiance over one hundred years ago, it was a promise all Americans intended to keep. When today's Americans pledge their allegiance to the flag of the United States of America, they mean what they say!

The stars and stripes blowing in the wind are a symbol of America's unity and pride.

Glossary

allegiance—loyalty of a citizen to his or her government

anonymous—without any name acknowledged (as an author of written work)

campaign—aggressive activities for a certain cause or purpose

civilians—people who aren't active employees of the government, military, police, or fire departments

convened—came together in a meeting or body

declaration—the act of declaring or announcing

Nazi—a member of the National Socialist German Workers' party of Germany

obligatory—required as a matter of obligation or compulsory (must do)

patriotism—love, support, loyalty, and defense of one's country

secede—to leave a political body or organization

slaves—people who are the property of or owned by another person

socialism—an economic and political system in which the land and means of production are owned by the public or government

theological seminary—a special school providing education in religion to prepare someone for the priesthood or ministry

unanimously—in complete agreement

waning—dying out

Timeline: The Pledge of

1845	1855	1865	1888	1892	1920	1923
James Bailey Upham is born.	Francis Bellamy is born.	The Civil War ends.	James Upham begins the campaign for a School Flag Movement.	The Pledge of Allegiance recited for first time on Columbus Day.	Women win the right to vote.	The words *my flag* are replaced by *the flag of the United States* in the Pledge of Allegiance.

1943	1954	1992	2001	
The Supreme Court rules that it is against the law to force anyone to recite the pledge.	The words *under God* are added to the pledge.	The Pledge of Allegiance is one hundred years old.	**SEPTEMBER 11** Terrorists attack the United States.	**OCTOBER 2001** The country pauses on Columbus Day and recites the Pledge of Allegiance.

Allegiance

1924	1929	1931	1939	1942

The Pledge of Allegiance is made a part of national law.

The words *of America* are added to the Pledge.	The final issue of *The Youth's Companion* is printed.	Francis Bellamy dies at age seventy-six.	Francis Bellamy is awarded authorship of the pledge.	

To Find Out More

BOOKS

Marsh, Carole. *The Young Patriot's Book of Puzzles, Games, Riddles, Stories, Poems, and Activities.* Peachtree City, GA: Gallopade Publishing Group, 2001.

Rife, Douglas M. *History Speaks: Pledge of Allegiance.* Carthage, IL: Teaching & Learning Company, 1998.

Schaefer, Lola M. *Symbols of Freedom: Pledge of Allegiance.* Portsmouth, NH: Heinemann Library, 2001.

ONLINE SITES

Federal Flag Code
http://usinfo.state.gov/usa/infousa/facts/symbols/flagcode.htm

The Flag of the United States
http://www.usflag.org/toc.html

The Pledge of Allegiance—A Centennial History 1892–1992
http://www.vineyard.net/vineyard/history/pdgech0.htm

A Short History of the Pledge
http://www.vineyard.net/vineyard/history/pledge.htm

Story and Meaning of the Pledge
http://www.flagday.org/Pages/StoryofPledge.htm

Index

About the Author

Christine Webster is a children's author with a special interest in U.S. history. Her work for Children's Press includes titles for the series From Sea to Shining Sea and Cornerstones of Freedom. She lives in Canada with her husband and four children.